barbarian businessman
(sacking and looting)

His wife Helga

Their problem son Hamlet
(he refuses to grow his hair to a
decent length, washes almost
daily, and reads books)

Their still unmarried daughter
Honi (she's 16)

And Hägar's sidekick,
Lucky Eddie—

Who collectively appear in close to 600
Sunday and daily papers, read by 35 million
people!

HÄGAR
THE HORRIBLE #2

BY DIK BROWNE

tempo books

GROSSET & DUNLAP, INC.
Publishers · New York

MY BEARD ISN'T ALL RED... THERE ARE TINY FLECKS OF SILVER AND GOLD IN IT!

DON'T YOU THINK THEY LOOK DISTINGUISHED?

THOSE ARE CODFISH FLAKES...

OH, WORDS OF LOVE
OH, WORDS DIVINE

THE SILVER THOUGHT THE GOLDEN LINE

OF ALL MEN'S WORDS THERE'S NONE SO FINE

AS THESE THREE WORDS...
"I GOT MINE"

IS IT POLITE TO EAT CHICKEN WITH YOUR FINGERS?

YES, IT'S QUITE POLITE TO EAT CHICKEN WITH YOUR FINGERS.

DIK·BROWNE 11-6

BUT ONLY AFTER IT'S COOKED, STUPID!

©King Features Syndicate Inc., 1974.

I GOT SOME GOOD NEWS AND SOME BAD NEWS — THE GALLEY IS ON FIRE AND WE'VE SPRUNG A LEAK.

2-26

WHAT'S THE GOOD NEWS?

ALL THE RATS HAVE LEFT THE SHIP.

DIK BROWNE